The Digital Revolution

Central Bank Digital Currencies (CBDC) Unveiled

BY
Michael McNaught

An educational book for readers of all ages.

Interested in learning about Central Bank Digital Currencies? Well, this is the book for you!

Preface

-Poem

In the realm of finance, a new dawn breaks,

A currency transformation, the ground it shakes.

Central Bank Digital Currency, known as CBDC,

A digital revolution, changing how we see.

No longer bound by physical notes and coins,

The future arrives with digital coins.

Central banks step forward, embracing the change,

A new era begins, it's time to rearrange.

With blockchain technology, secure and strong,

CBDC emerges, where trust belongs.

Transparency and speed, the driving force,

Empowering transactions with a digital course.

No borders or boundaries, it knows no bounds,

CBDC connects nations, their economies astound.

Instantaneous transfers, without a delay,

A global currency, breaking barriers away.

The power to include the unbanked, the ones left behind,

CBDC reaches far and wide, a remedy to find.

Financial inclusion, a noble quest,

CBDC offers hope, giving everyone their best.

Privacy and security, concerns held dear,

CBDC safeguards, alleviating any fear.

With encryption and protocols, protection is assured,

Your digital wealth, safely secured.

But challenges lie ahead, as progress unfolds,

Adapting to the future, embracing what it holds.

Educating the masses, embracing the new,

CBDC paves the way, revealing a breakthrough.

Central Bank Digital Currency, a transformative dream,

Reinventing the system, a progressive theme.

With each digital transaction, a step into the unknown,

CBDC heralds change, a currency to be shown.

Hi there! My name is Michael McNaught, a scientist by profession, and an avid blockchain and digital currency enthusiast. I enjoy learning about this amazing cutting-edge technology and sharing my knowledge with others.

In the vast landscape of financial systems, a quiet yet profound revolution is underway, one that has the potential to reshape the way we perceive and interact with money. The advent of Central Bank Digital Currencies (CBDCs) marks a significant milestone in the evolution of currency, challenging conventional notions of monetary transactions and ushering in a new era of digital finance.

If you are interested in learning about this new monetary system, CBDC, well look no further! This is the book for you! I do hope that by reading this book you learn something new, informative and valuable. For purchasing this book, I thank you!

Table of Contents

Chapter 1:

Introduction to Central Bank Digital Currencies

Section 1: Understanding the Need for Digital Currencies

In today's rapidly evolving digital landscape, traditional financial systems face new challenges and opportunities. As technological advancements reshape the way we conduct transactions, there is a growing need for digital currencies to address the limitations of traditional forms of money. This section explores the reasons behind the increasing demand for digital currencies and their potential benefits.

1.1 Advancements in Technology

The digital revolution has transformed various aspects of our lives, including how we exchange value. With the widespread availability of the internet, smartphones, and other digital devices, people are increasingly seeking faster, more convenient, and secure ways to make transactions. Digital currencies leverage these technological advancements to provide a seamless digital payment experience, eliminating the need for physical cash or traditional banking systems.

1.2 Globalization and Cross-Border Transactions

In an interconnected world, cross-border transactions are becoming more common. Traditional payment systems often involve complex processes, intermediaries, and high fees, making international transactions time-consuming and costly. Digital currencies have the potential to simplify cross-border transactions, enabling faster and more cost-effective transfers without the need for intermediaries. This can significantly improve financial inclusion and facilitate global trade and economic growth.

1.3 Financial Inclusion

A significant portion of the global population remains unbanked or underbanked, lacking access to basic financial services. Traditional banking systems often have barriers such as high transaction fees, minimum balance requirements, and limited accessibility, preventing many individuals from participating fully in the economy. Digital currencies, particularly those built on decentralized technologies, offer an opportunity to provide financial services to the unbanked and underbanked populations, empowering them with secure and affordable means of storing, transferring, and managing their funds.

1.4 Security and Transparency

Digital currencies can enhance the security and transparency of transactions. Traditional cash transactions are susceptible to theft, counterfeiting, and loss. Digital currencies, on the other hand, utilize cryptographic algorithms and decentralized ledger technologies like blockchain to secure transactions. These technologies provide strong encryption and immutability, ensuring that transactions are tamper-proof and traceable. By enhancing security and transparency, digital currencies can help combat fraud, money laundering, and other illicit activities.

1.5 Financial Innovation and Economic Growth

Digital currencies have the potential to spur financial innovation and foster economic growth. They provide a platform for the development of new financial products and services, such as decentralized lending, smart contracts, and programmable money. These innovations can streamline business processes, reduce transaction costs, and enable new forms of economic collaboration. Additionally, the adoption of digital currencies

an attract investment and stimulate economic activity by creating a
more efficient and inclusive financial ecosystem.

1.6 Addressing the Limitations of Traditional Banking Systems

Traditional banking systems often have limitations that hinder financial
inclusion and access to services. These limitations include limited
operating hours, high fees, cumbersome bureaucracy, and geographical
constraints. Digital currencies can overcome these limitations by
operating 24/7, offering lower transaction costs, reducing paperwork,
and enabling borderless transactions. As a result, individuals and
businesses can have greater control over their finances and access to a
wider range of financial services.

Section 2: Brief History of Money and Its Evolution

Money, in its various forms, has played a crucial role in human
civilization for thousands of years. This section provides a brief
overview of the history of money, highlighting its evolution from
primitive forms of exchange to the modern digital currencies we see
today.

2.1 Barter and Commodity Money

Before the advent of money, people relied on bartering to exchange
goods and services. Barter involves the direct exchange of one good for
another without the need for a common medium of exchange. While
bartering allowed individuals to acquire what they needed, it had
limitations. The lack of a standardized measure of value and the
difficulty of finding parties willing to trade created challenges.

To overcome these challenges, societies began using commodity money.
Commodity money took the form of objects that had inherent value, such
as shells, salt, livestock, or precious metals. These items were widely
accepted as a medium of exchange due to their usefulness, scarcity, and
durability. Commodity money simplified transactions by providing a
standardized measure of value and acting as a store of wealth.

2.2 The Introduction of Coins and Paper Currency

With the rise of civilizations, the need for a more standardized and convenient form of money became evident. Around 600 BCE, the Lydians in present-day Turkey introduced the world's first coins made from electrum, a natural alloy of gold and silver. Coins revolutionized the concept of money by providing a portable, divisible, and widely accepted medium of exchange. They had standardized weights and measures, making transactions more efficient and reliable.

In the 11th century, China introduced the first paper currency. Paper money, initially used as a representation of precious metals held in reserve, offered a more convenient alternative to carrying bulky coins. This innovation marked a significant shift toward using representative money, where the currency's value was backed by a commodity, typically gold or silver.

2.3 Fiat Currency and the Modern Banking System

The development of modern banking systems in the 17th century brought about a new era in the evolution of money. Governments gradually transitioned from using commodity-backed money to fiat currency. Fiat currency derives its value from the trust and confidence people place in the issuing authority, typically the government or central bank.

Fiat currency enabled governments to have greater control over monetary policy and the supply of money. It facilitated economic growth, as governments could issue currency without being limited by the availability of precious metals. This era also witnessed the establishment of central banks, which were responsible for managing the monetary system, maintaining price stability, and acting as lenders of last resort.

2.4 Digital Money and the Rise of Cryptocurrencies

With the advent of the internet and electronic payment systems in the late 20th century, digital money emerged as a new form of currency. Initially, digital money represented traditional fiat currencies stored

4

lectronically in banks or payment systems. It facilitated online ransactions, offering convenience and speed.

n 2009, the introduction of Bitcoin, the first decentralized ryptocurrency, marked a significant turning point in the evolution of noney. Bitcoin, built on blockchain technology, eliminated the need for ntermediaries and provided a secure, transparent, and decentralized ystem for conducting transactions. Bitcoin's success paved the way for he proliferation of cryptocurrencies, each with its unique features and ıse cases.

Section 3: Exploring the Concept of Central Bank Digital Currencies CBDCs)

3.1 Definition and Features of CBDCs

Central Bank Digital Currency (CBDC) can be defined as a digital form of a nation's currency, issued and regulated by the country's central bank. t serves as a digital representation of the national currency, aiming to provide a secure and efficient medium of exchange for both individuals and businesses. CBDCs are designed to operate within a controlled and regulated framework, differentiating them from decentralized cryptocurrencies.

CBDCs leverage advanced technologies such as blockchain or distributed ledger technology (DLT) to ensure secure and transparent transactions. These technologies enable the recording and verification of every transaction, ensuring that the system remains trustworthy and resistant to fraud.

3.2 Motivations for CBDCs

The development and implementation of CBDCs are driven by a range of motivations and objectives that vary across countries. Some of the common motivations include:

- Financial Inclusion: CBDCs can promote greater financial inclusion by providing access to digital financial services to unbanked and underbanked populations.
- Payment System Efficiency: CBDCs can enhance the speed, efficiency, and security of payment systems, enabling real-time transactions and reducing reliance on intermediaries.
- Monetary Policy and Financial Stability: CBDCs provide central banks with more direct control over monetary policy, facilitating efficient transmission mechanisms and enhancing financial stability.
- Counteracting Private Cryptocurrencies: CBDCs offer a regulated alternative to private cryptocurrencies, addressing concerns related to consumer protection, money laundering, and financial stability.
- Innovation and Technological Advancement: CBDCs can foster innovation in financial services and support the development of new digital payment solutions, such as smart contracts and programmable money.

Section 4: Different Types of CBDCs and Their Characteristics

4.1 Retail CBDCs

Retail CBDCs are designed for direct use by individuals and businesses for everyday transactions. They are similar to traditional cash or electronic money, providing a digital representation of the national currency. Retail CBDCs aim to enhance financial inclusion, improve payment system efficiency, and provide a secure and convenient means of exchange for the general public.

4.2 Wholesale CBDCs

Wholesale CBDCs, also known as interbank or institutional CBDCs, are designed for use by financial institutions, central banks, and other eligible entities. Wholesale CBDCs facilitate large-scale interbank transactions, settlement processes, and the implementation of monetary policy. They can enhance the efficiency and resilience of financial markets, reducing settlement risks and improving liquidity management.

4.3 Hybrid CBDCs

Hybrid CBDCs combine features of both retail and wholesale CBDCs. They cater to the needs of both individuals and financial institutions, providing a versatile digital currency solution. Hybrid CBDCs aim to strike a balance between retail accessibility and institutional functionality, offering a wide range of use cases across the economy.

In summary, this chapter provided an understanding of the need for digital currencies, traced the evolution of money from barter to digital forms, explored the concept of Central Bank Digital Currencies (CBDCs), and discussed different types of CBDCs and their characteristics. The subsequent chapters will delve deeper into the implementation, benefits, challenges, and implications of CBDCs on the global financial landscape.

Chapter 2:

The Role of Central Banks in the Digital Age

Section 1: The Changing Landscape of Central Banking

The digital age has brought about significant changes in the financial landscape, necessitating the adaptation of central banks to new technological advancements and evolving market dynamics. This section examines the transformation of central banking in the digital age and the challenges and opportunities it presents.

1.1 Evolving Financial Systems

Digitalization has disrupted traditional financial systems, altering the way individuals and businesses transact, save, and invest. The rise of digital payments, online banking, and cryptocurrencies has reshaped the financial ecosystem, demanding a proactive response from central banks. Central banks are reevaluating their roles and responsibilities to ensure the effectiveness of monetary policy, financial stability, and consumer protection in the digital era.

1.2 Technological Advancements

Technological advancements, such as blockchain, artificial intelligence, and big data analytics, have the potential to revolutionize financial services. Central banks are exploring the applications of these technologies to enhance their operations, improve payment systems, and address emerging risks. The integration of technology into central banking practices can lead to greater efficiency, transparency, and resilience in the financial system.

1.3 Regulatory Challenges

The digital age has also presented new regulatory challenges for central banks. The proliferation of cryptocurrencies, initial coin offerings (ICOs), and decentralized financial platforms has raised concerns about consumer protection, financial integrity, and the stability of the financial system. Central banks are actively working to develop regulatory frameworks that strike a balance between fostering innovation and safeguarding financial stability.

Section 2: The Motivations Behind Central Banks Issuing Digital Currencies

Central banks worldwide are exploring the issuance of Central Bank Digital Currencies (CBDCs) with specific motivations and objectives. This section explores the various factors that drive central banks to consider the introduction of CBDCs.

2.1 Enhancing Payment Systems

One of the primary motivations for central banks to issue CBDCs is to enhance payment systems. CBDCs can provide a secure, efficient, and inclusive digital payment infrastructure, reducing reliance on cash and traditional payment methods. By offering instant and low-cost transactions, CBDCs can promote financial inclusion, streamline cross-border payments, and reduce settlement risks.

2.2 Ensuring Monetary Sovereignty

CBDCs can safeguard a central bank's control over monetary sovereignty in an increasingly digital and globalized world. By providing a digital form of legal tender issued by the central bank, CBDCs enable direct and secure transactions that align with the central bank's monetary policy objectives. CBDCs can also mitigate the potential risks associated

with private digital currencies that may challenge the central bank'
authority over the monetary system.

2.3 Promoting Financial Inclusion

Financial inclusion is a significant motivation behind the issuance o:
CBDCs. By leveraging digital technologies, CBDCs can provide acces:
to basic financial services for individuals who are unbanked o
underserved by traditional banking systems. CBDCs can empowe
individuals with secure and affordable means of storing, transferring, anc
managing their funds, fostering economic participation and reducing
economic disparities.

2.4 Addressing Privacy and Security Concerns

Privacy and security are paramount considerations for central banks in
the digital age. CBDCs can be designed with advanced encryption and
privacy features to protect user data while ensuring regulatory
compliance. By offering a trusted and secure digital payment solution,
CBDCs can address concerns related to data breaches, identity theft, and
fraud, providing individuals with greater control over their financial
information.

Section 3: Assessing the Potential Benefits and Risks of CBDCs

The issuance of CBDCs holds the potential for numerous benefits, but it
also entails certain risks and challenges. This section examines the
potential advantages and risks associated with CBDCs.

3.1 Potential Benefits of CBDCs

- Improved Payment Efficiency: CBDCs can enable real-time,
  low-cost, and secure transactions, reducing reliance on
  intermediaries and enhancing payment system efficiency.
- Financial Inclusion: CBDCs can extend financial services to
  unbanked and underbanked populations, promoting inclusive
  economic growth.

- Enhanced Monetary Policy Tools: CBDCs provide central banks with direct access to data on transactions, enabling better monitoring and analysis for more effective monetary policy implementation.
- Reduced Transaction Costs: CBDCs can streamline cross-border transactions, reducing transaction costs and enhancing international trade.
- Counteracting Private Cryptocurrencies: CBDCs can offer a regulated alternative to private cryptocurrencies, mitigating risks related to consumer protection, money laundering, and financial stability.

.2 Potential Risks and Challenges of CBDCs

- Technological Risks: CBDCs rely on advanced technologies, which may be vulnerable to cyber threats, hacking, or system failures, requiring robust security measures and infrastructure.
- Privacy Concerns: The collection and management of user data in CBDC systems may raise privacy concerns, necessitating the implementation of privacy-enhancing measures and strict data protection regulations.
- Financial Stability Risks: The introduction of CBDCs may impact the stability of the financial system, requiring careful consideration of potential risks, such as bank disintermediation, liquidity risks, and systemic vulnerabilities.
- Operational Challenges: The implementation of CBDCs involves complex operational challenges, including scalability, interoperability, governance, and legal considerations, necessitating thorough planning and collaboration among stakeholders.

Section 4: Impact on Monetary Policy, Financial Stability, and Economic Development

The introduction of CBDCs has significant implications for monetary policy, financial stability, and economic development. This section examines the potential impacts of CBDCs in these key areas.

4.1 Monetary Policy Implementation

CBDCs can provide central banks with enhanced tools for monetary policy implementation. The direct access to transaction data and real time insights offered by CBDCs can improve the effectiveness of monetary policy decisions, allowing central banks to monitor economic activity, manage inflation, and respond swiftly to changing economic conditions.

4.2 Financial Stability

CBDCs can contribute to financial stability by reducing counterparty and settlement risks, enhancing transparency, and promoting sound financial practices. However, the introduction of CBDCs must be carefully managed to mitigate potential risks, such as bank disintermediation, digital runs, and financial contagion.

4.3 Economic Development

CBDCs have the potential to foster economic development by promoting financial inclusion, reducing transaction costs, and increasing access to digital financial services. CBDCs can support economic growth, facilitate cross-border trade, and improve efficiency in financial transactions, benefitting both individuals and businesses.

In conclusion, central banks are adapting to the digital age by exploring the issuance of CBDCs. Motivated by various factors, including the need for enhanced payment systems, monetary sovereignty, financial inclusion, and privacy and security concerns, central banks are assessing the potential benefits and risks of CBDCs. The implementation of CBDCs can impact monetary policy, financial stability, and economic development, requiring careful consideration of technological, regulatory, and operational challenges.

Chapter 3:

Technological Foundations of CBDCs

Section 1: The Underlying Technologies behind CBDCs (Blockchain, Distributed Ledger Technology)

Central Bank Digital Currencies (CBDCs) leverage advanced technologies to provide secure and efficient digital payment solutions. This section explores the underlying technologies commonly associated with CBDCs, namely blockchain and distributed ledger technology (DLT).

1.1 Blockchain Technology

Blockchain is a decentralized and immutable digital ledger that records transactions across multiple computers or nodes. It operates through a consensus mechanism, ensuring the transparency and integrity of data. In the context of CBDCs, blockchain technology can provide a secure and transparent platform for recording and verifying transactions.

By utilizing blockchain, CBDCs can offer benefits such as:

- Security: Blockchain employs cryptographic techniques to secure transactions, making them tamper-resistant and reducing the risk of fraud.
- Transparency: The transparent nature of blockchain allows participants to independently verify transactions, enhancing trust and accountability.

- Resilience: Blockchain's distributed nature ensures that no single point of failure exists, making the system more resilient to attacks and disruptions.

1.2 Distributed Ledger Technology (DLT)

DLT is a broader term that encompasses various distributed database technologies, including blockchain. DLT offers a decentralized and shared database where participants can securely record, store, and validate transactions. Unlike traditional centralized databases, DLT enables multiple parties to maintain copies of the ledger, promoting transparency and reducing reliance on intermediaries.

DLT can provide the following advantages for CBDCs:

- Decentralization: DLT eliminates the need for a central authority, enabling peer-to-peer transactions and reducing dependency on intermediaries.
- Efficiency: DLT facilitates near real-time settlement and reduces the complexity and costs associated with traditional clearing and settlement processes.
- Scalability: Some DLT solutions offer scalability improvements, allowing for higher transaction throughput to accommodate the demands of a digital currency system.

Section 2: Advantages and Challenges Associated with Implementing Blockchain-based CBDCs

2.1 Advantages of Blockchain-based CBDCs

Implementing CBDCs using blockchain technology offers several potential advantages:

- Security and Immutability: Blockchain's cryptographic mechanisms make it highly secure, reducing the risk of counterfeiting and fraud. Once recorded, transactions on the blockchain are virtually immutable, ensuring the integrity of the transaction history.

14

- Transparency and Auditability: Blockchain's transparent nature allows for enhanced transparency and auditability of transactions, providing a high level of trust and accountability.
- Efficiency and Speed: Blockchain-based CBDCs can facilitate near-instantaneous transactions, eliminating the need for intermediaries and reducing settlement times.
- Programmability: Smart contract functionality embedded in blockchain can enable programmable money, allowing for automated and self-executing transactions with predefined conditions.

2.2 Challenges of Blockchain-based CBDCs

Implementing blockchain-based CBDCs also presents certain challenges that need to be addressed:

- Scalability: Traditional blockchain architectures may struggle to handle the high transaction volumes required for a national-scale digital currency. Achieving the necessary scalability while maintaining decentralization and security remains a challenge.
- Privacy: Blockchain's transparency can pose challenges in preserving the privacy of CBDC transactions. Striking a balance between transparency and user privacy is crucial in designing a blockchain-based CBDC.
- Governance and Legal Frameworks: Establishing governance frameworks and legal structures for blockchain-based CBDCs require careful consideration. Issues such as regulatory compliance, identity verification, and dispute resolution mechanisms need to be addressed.

Section 3: Alternative Approaches to CBDCs and Their Technological Implications

3.1 Centralized Database Approach

While blockchain and DLT are commonly associated with CBDCs, alternative approaches utilizing centralized databases are also being considered. In a centralized database approach, the central bank maintains control over the issuance, distribution, and validation of the CBDC. This approach offers greater control and scalability, but it may sacrifice some of the decentralization and transparency benefit associated with blockchain-based CBDCs.

3.2 Tokenization and Interoperability

Another technological consideration for CBDCs is tokenization, where CBDCs are represented as digital tokens on a blockchain or DLT platform. Tokenization allows for improved interoperability, enabling seamless transactions between different CBDCs or even private digital currencies. However, achieving interoperability among different CBDC systems and private cryptocurrencies requires standardized protocols and regulatory frameworks.

In conclusion, the technological foundations of CBDCs primarily rely on blockchain and distributed ledger technology. These technologies offer advantages such as security, transparency, and efficiency. However, implementing blockchain-based CBDCs presents challenges related to scalability, privacy, and governance. Additionally, alternative approaches utilizing centralized databases and considerations like tokenization and interoperability need to be explored. Careful evaluation of the technological options is crucial to ensure the successful implementation of CBDCs while addressing the unique requirements and objectives of central banks.

Chapter 4:

Global Perspectives on CBDCs

Section 1: Analyzing CBDC Initiatives across Different Countries

Central Bank Digital Currencies (CBDCs) have garnered significant attention worldwide, with many countries actively exploring or piloting CBDC projects. This section provides an analysis of CBDC initiatives across different countries, highlighting their motivations, progress, and key considerations.

1.1 Motivations for CBDC Implementation

Countries have diverse motivations for considering CBDC implementation, including:

- Financial Inclusion: Some countries aim to extend financial services to unbanked and underbanked populations, leveraging CBDCs to promote inclusive economic growth.
- Payment System Modernization: Countries seek to enhance payment system efficiency, security, and cost-effectiveness by leveraging CBDCs as a digital form of central bank money.
- Technological Innovation: CBDCs present an opportunity for countries to embrace technological advancements, such as blockchain or distributed ledger technology, fostering innovation in financial services.
- Monetary Policy Enhancement: CBDCs can provide central banks with new tools for monetary policy implementation, enabling better monitoring of transactions and enhancing policy effectiveness.

1.2 Progress and Pilots

Countries have made varying degrees of progress in CBDC developmen and implementation. Some have conducted pilot projects an experiments to assess the feasibility and impact of CBDCs. Notabl examples include the Bahamas' Sand Dollar, China's Digital Yuar Sweden's e-krona, and the Eastern Caribbean Central Bank's DCash These pilot projects provide valuable insights into the potential benefits challenges, and user experiences of CBDCs.

Section 2: Case Studies of Successful CBDC Implementations

2.1 The Bahamas: Sand Dollar

The Sand Dollar, launched by the Central Bank of The Bahamas, is one of the world's first fully deployed CBDCs. It aims to address challenges related to financial inclusion and payment system efficiency. The Sand Dollar has facilitated digital transactions, reduced reliance on cash, and enhanced financial services access for remote communities.

2.2 China: Digital Yuan (e-CNY)

China has been at the forefront of CBDC development with its Digital Yuan, also known as the e-CNY. The Digital Yuan has undergone extensive testing and pilot programs across various cities. It aims to modernize China's payment systems, enhance financial inclusion, and provide the central bank with improved tools for monetary policy implementation.

2.3 Sweden: e-krona

Sweden's Riksbank has been exploring the issuance of the e-krona to address the decline in cash usage and ensure a resilient payment infrastructure. The e-krona project focuses on user-friendliness, security, and efficiency. It aims to provide a digital complement to cash, ensuring the availability of central bank money for all citizens.

Section 3: Comparative Analysis of Different Approaches and Strategies

3.1 Design Choices and Technological Solutions

Countries adopt different design choices and technological solutions for their CBDCs. These choices include the use of blockchain or DLT, the level of privacy and anonymity, the degree of centralization or decentralization, and the integration with existing payment systems. Comparative analysis helps identify the trade-offs and implications of various approaches.

3.2 User Adoption and Acceptance

Understanding user adoption and acceptance is crucial for successful CBDC implementation. Factors influencing user adoption include user experience, accessibility, trust, education, and incentives. Comparative analysis of different countries' approaches can provide insights into effective strategies for fostering user adoption and acceptance of CBDCs.

Section 4: Cross-Border Implications and Potential Challenges

4.1 Interoperability and Cross-Border Payments

CBDCs have implications for cross-border payments, including interoperability challenges and potential impacts on existing payment systems. Harmonization of standards and protocols is essential to ensure efficient cross-border transactions and interoperability between different CBDC systems.

4.2 Regulatory and Legal Considerations

Cross-border implementation of CBDCs necessitates addressing regulatory and legal considerations, including anti-money laundering (AML) and know-your-customer (KYC) requirements, data privacy, jurisdictional challenges, and harmonization of international regulations. Collaboration among central banks and regulatory bodies is essential to address these challenges effectively.

4.3 Geopolitical and Economic Implications

CBDCs may have geopolitical and economic implications, including changes in monetary sovereignty, the role of reserve currencies, and the international monetary system. Analyzing these implications can provide insights into potential challenges and opportunities for countries implementing CBDCs.

In conclusion, CBDC initiatives vary across countries, reflecting unique motivations, progress, and considerations. Case studies of successful CBDC implementations, such as the Bahamas' Sand Dollar, China's Digital Yuan, and Sweden's e-krona, offer valuable insights. Comparative analysis helps evaluate different approaches, design choices, and user adoption strategies. Cross-border implications and challenges, including interoperability, regulatory considerations, and geopolitical impacts, require collaborative efforts and careful considerations by central banks and regulatory bodies.

Chapter 5:

Designing and Implementing CBDCs

Section 1: Legal and Regulatory Considerations for CBDC Implementation

Designing and implementing Central Bank Digital Currencies (CBDCs) involve navigating various legal and regulatory considerations. This section explores key aspects that central banks and policymakers need to address during the development and deployment of CBDCs.

1.1 Regulatory Frameworks and Compliance

Developing a robust regulatory framework is crucial to ensure the successful implementation of CBDCs. This framework should address issues such as anti-money laundering (AML), know-your-customer (KYC) requirements, consumer protection, privacy regulations, and cybersecurity measures. Collaboration between central banks, financial regulators, and other relevant authorities is essential to establish an effective and comprehensive regulatory framework.

1.2 Legal Implications and Jurisdictional Challenges

Implementing CBDCs raises legal implications and jurisdictional challenges, especially in cross-border transactions. It requires clarity on the legal status of CBDCs, contract enforceability, jurisdictional authority, and dispute resolution mechanisms. International cooperation and harmonization of laws and regulations are crucial to address these challenges and ensure smooth cross-border CBDC operations.

Section 2: Privacy and Security Concerns Surrounding Digital Currencies

2.1 Privacy Considerations

Preserving user privacy is a critical aspect of CBDC design. While transparency and accountability are essential, striking a balance with individual privacy rights is crucial. CBDC systems should incorporate privacy-enhancing technologies, such as zero-knowledge proofs or selective disclosure mechanisms, to protect user information. Implementing robust data protection regulations and ensuring secure data storage and transmission are also necessary to address privacy concerns.

2.2 Security Measures

CBDCs must be designed with stringent security measures to protect against cyber threats, hacking, and fraud. Implementing robust encryption techniques, multi-factor authentication, secure key management systems, and regular security audits are essential. Collaborating with cybersecurity experts and adopting industry best practices can help ensure the integrity and resilience of CBDC systems.

Section 3: User Adoption and Accessibility Challenges

3.1 User Experience and Education

Ensuring a seamless user experience is crucial for user adoption of CBDCs. CBDC systems should be designed with user-friendly interfaces and intuitive functionalities. Additionally, providing educational resources to users, including information on how to use CBDCs securely and understand their benefits, is essential to drive adoption.

3.2 Financial Inclusion and Accessibility

CBDCs can play a significant role in promoting financial inclusion, but it is essential to address accessibility challenges. Ensuring that CBDCs are accessible to all segments of society, including those with limited igital literacy or physical disabilities, is crucial. Collaborating with inancial institutions, payment service providers, and other stakeholders an help ensure widespread accessibility of CBDCs.

Section 4: Interoperability and Standardization in the CBDC Ecosystem

4.1 Interoperability Challenges

nteroperability is vital for the seamless functioning of CBDCs, especially in cross-border transactions. Harmonizing technical tandards, protocols, and governance frameworks across different CBDC systems is crucial to enable interoperability. Collaborative efforts among central banks, standardization bodies, and international organizations can help establish interoperability in the CBDC ecosystem.

4.2 International Cooperation and Standardization

Promoting international cooperation and standardization is essential to facilitate interoperability and foster trust in CBDCs. Collaborative initiatives, such as cross-border pilot projects and information sharing platforms, can promote knowledge exchange, harmonize regulations, and establish common standards. Engaging with international organizations, such as the International Monetary Fund (IMF) and the Financial Stability Board (FSB), can facilitate global coordination in CBDC design and implementation.

In conclusion, designing and implementing CBDCs require careful consideration of legal and regulatory frameworks, privacy and security measures, user adoption strategies, and interoperability standards. Establishing robust regulatory frameworks, addressing privacy concerns, ensuring security measures, fostering user adoption, and promoting interoperability are essential for the successful implementation of CBDCs. Collaboration among central banks, policymakers, financial institutions, and international organizations is crucial to address the challenges and seize the opportunities presented by CBDCs.

Chapter 6:

Implications for Financial Institutions and Payment Systems

Section 1: Impact on Commercial Banks and Traditional Financial Intermediation

The introduction of Central Bank Digital Currencies (CBDCs) has significant implications for commercial banks and traditional financial intermediation.

1.1 Reshaping the Banking Landscape

CBDCs have the potential to reshape the banking landscape by altering the relationship between central banks and commercial banks. As CBDCs provide a digital form of central bank money, they may reduce the demand for traditional bank deposits, affecting banks' ability to generate interest income and fund their lending activities.

1.2 Changes in Business Models

Commercial banks may need to adapt their business models to incorporate CBDCs. They can explore opportunities in providing value-added services, such as custodial services, digital wallets, and financial advisory services, to differentiate themselves in the CBDC ecosystem. Collaboration with fintech firms and technology providers can enable banks to leverage their expertise and infrastructure in delivering innovative solutions.

Section 2: Potential Disruption to the Existing Payment Systems

The introduction of CBDCs has the potential to disrupt existing payment systems, including both domestic and cross-border transactions.

2.1 Increased Competition and Efficiency

CBDCs can enhance payment system efficiency by enabling real-time settlements, reducing transaction costs, and improving transparency. This increased efficiency may challenge traditional payment systems, such as card networks and legacy cross-border remittance services, by offering faster and cheaper alternatives.

2.2 Financial Inclusion and Access

CBDCs can play a crucial role in advancing financial inclusion by providing individuals and businesses with access to digital payment infrastructure, particularly in underserved areas. This may pose challenges for existing payment service providers to adapt and cater to the evolving needs of a more inclusive and digitally enabled economy.

Section 3: Addressing the Risks of Financial Disintermediation

The introduction of CBDCs raises concerns about potential financial disintermediation, where individuals and businesses may prefer to hold CBDCs directly with the central bank, bypassing commercial banks.

3.1 Mitigating Systemic Risks

Financial authorities and central banks need to carefully evaluate and address the systemic risks associated with potential disintermediation. Maintaining financial stability, ensuring liquidity management, and preserving the effectiveness of monetary policy transmission are critical considerations.

3.2 Designing Incentives for Collaboration

To mitigate the risks of disintermediation, central banks can design CBDC frameworks that incentivize collaboration between central banks and commercial banks. This can involve providing commercial banks with access to CBDCs, allowing them to offer value-added services, or establishing partnerships that leverage the strengths of both central banks and commercial banks in delivering financial services.

Section 4: Collaborative Approaches Between Central Banks and Commercial Banks

4.1 Public-Private Partnerships

Collaboration between central banks and commercial banks is crucial to ensure the smooth integration of CBDCs into the existing financial ecosystem. Public-private partnerships can facilitate knowledge sharing, promote innovation, and address common challenges related to CBDC implementation, such as identity verification, cybersecurity, and interoperability.

4.2 Leveraging Existing Expertise

Commercial banks bring extensive expertise in customer relationship management, risk management, and financial services delivery. Central banks can leverage this expertise by working closely with commercial banks to develop innovative solutions, streamline processes, and enhance the overall user experience of CBDCs.

In conclusion, the introduction of CBDCs has far-reaching implications for financial institutions and payment systems. Commercial banks will need to adapt their business models to the changing landscape, while payment systems may undergo significant transformations. Collaboration between central banks and commercial banks is essential to address the risks associated with financial disintermediation and ensure the successful integration of CBDCs into the existing financial ecosystem.

Chapter 7:
CBDCs and Financial Inclusion

Section 1: The Potential of CBDCs to Promote Financial Inclusion

Central Bank Digital Currencies (CBDCs) hold significant potential in advancing financial inclusion by addressing barriers and expanding access to financial services for underserved populations.

1.1 Enhanced Access to Payment Services

CBDCs can provide individuals and businesses with a secure and convenient means of accessing payment services. By leveraging digital technologies, CBDCs enable instant and low-cost transactions, reducing reliance on cash and traditional banking infrastructure. This accessibility empowers individuals who previously lacked access to formal financial services.

1.2 Inclusion of Unbanked and Underbanked Populations

CBDCs can extend financial services to unbanked and underbanked populations, who may face challenges in accessing traditional banking services. CBDCs offer an opportunity to bridge the gap, allowing individuals to hold and transact in digital currencies directly with the central bank, bypassing the need for a traditional bank account.

Section 2: Addressing the Digital Divide and Accessibility Challenges

2.1 Overcoming Infrastructure Limitations

CBDCs can help address infrastructure limitations in underserved areas. As CBDCs operate on digital platforms, they can leverage existing telecommunications and mobile networks to provide financial services in regions with limited physical banking infrastructure.

2.2 Digital Literacy and Education

Promoting digital literacy and providing education about CBDCs are vital components of ensuring financial inclusion. Efforts should be made to educate individuals on how to use CBDCs securely, understand their benefits, and navigate digital interfaces. Collaboration among central banks, governments, and educational institutions can facilitate the dissemination of knowledge and skills required for effective CBDC adoption.

Section 3: Leveraging CBDCs for Poverty Reduction and Economic Empowerment

3.1 Microfinance and Micropayments

CBDCs can facilitate microfinance and micropayments, allowing for small-value transactions and enabling entrepreneurs in informal sectors to access financial services. By reducing transaction costs and increasing efficiency, CBDCs can empower individuals to participate more fully in the formal economy and unlock economic opportunities.

3.2 Social Welfare and Government Disbursements

CBDCs can enhance the delivery of social welfare programs and government disbursements. By digitizing these payments, CBDCs enable faster and more transparent distribution, reducing leakages and ensuring that funds reach the intended beneficiaries directly.

ection 4: Lessons Learned from Pilot Programs and Experiments

.1 Pilot Programs and Experiments

everal countries have conducted pilot programs and experiments to ssess the impact of CBDCs on financial inclusion. Lessons learned from hese initiatives provide valuable insights into the potential benefits, hallenges, and user experiences of CBDCs. Examples include the mplementation of CBDCs in rural or remote areas, collaboration with ocal communities, and measuring the socioeconomic impact of CBDC doption.

.2 Stakeholder Engagement and Feedback

Engaging with stakeholders, including underserved communities, inancial institutions, fintech companies, and non-governmental organizations, is crucial in designing inclusive CBDC frameworks. Soliciting feedback and incorporating the perspectives of different stakeholders can help shape CBDC policies and implementation strategies that address the specific needs of marginalized populations.

In conclusion, CBDCs have the potential to significantly advance financial inclusion by enhancing access to payment services, including unbanked populations, and addressing the digital divide. By overcoming infrastructure limitations, promoting digital literacy, and leveraging CBDCs for poverty reduction and economic empowerment, societies can create more inclusive and sustainable financial systems. Lessons learned from pilot programs and stakeholder engagement play a vital role in designing effective CBDC initiatives that prioritize financial inclusion.

Chapter 8:

Privacy, Security, and Regulatory Considerations

Section 1: Balancing Privacy and Financial Transparency in CBDCs

Central Bank Digital Currencies (CBDCs) raise important considerations regarding privacy and financial transparency. Striking the right balance between these two aspects is crucial to ensure the successful implementation and adoption of CBDCs.

1.1 Privacy-Preserving Design

CBDC systems should incorporate privacy-enhancing features to protect user information while maintaining the necessary level of transparency to prevent illicit activities. Techniques such as zero-knowledge proofs, selective disclosure mechanisms, and transactional privacy can be employed to safeguard individual privacy rights.

1.2 AML and KYC Compliance

While privacy is important, combating money laundering, terrorist financing, and other illicit activities remains a priority. CBDCs should be designed to comply with robust Anti-Money Laundering (AML) and Know-Your-Customer (KYC) regulations, ensuring transparency and accountability without compromising user privacy.

Section 2: Ensuring Robust Security Measures to Prevent Cyber Threats

2.1 Cybersecurity Infrastructure

CBDCs must prioritize cybersecurity to protect against potential cyber threats. Robust encryption, secure key management systems, and multi-factor authentication are essential security measures. Regular security audits, intrusion detection systems, and incident response protocols should be in place to detect and mitigate risks effectively.

2.2 Collaboration with Cybersecurity Experts

Collaboration with cybersecurity experts, both within the public and private sectors, is crucial to establish best practices and maintain the resilience of CBDC systems. Sharing threat intelligence, conducting penetration testing, and continuous monitoring are essential components of a comprehensive security strategy.

Section 3: Regulatory Frameworks for CBDCs and Combating Illicit Activities

3.1 AML/CFT Regulations

Regulatory frameworks for CBDCs should include comprehensive Anti-Money Laundering (AML) and Combating the Financing of Terrorism (CFT) measures. This involves establishing robust customer due diligence processes, transaction monitoring systems, and reporting mechanisms to detect and prevent illicit activities.

3.2 Regulatory Oversight and Compliance

Central banks and relevant regulatory authorities must ensure proper oversight and compliance with regulatory frameworks governing CBDCs. This includes regular audits, supervision of participants in the CBDC ecosystem, and enforcement of compliance standards to maintain the integrity and stability of the financial system.

Section 4: International Cooperation and Regulatory Coordination

4.1 Harmonization of Standards

Given the global nature of financial transactions, international cooperation and coordination among regulatory authorities are essential. Harmonizing standards and regulations related to CBDCs can help address cross-border challenges, ensure interoperability, and promote a level playing field.

4.2 Information Sharing and Collaboration

Central banks and regulatory authorities should actively engage in information sharing and collaboration to combat illicit activities facilitated by CBDCs. Sharing best practices, intelligence, and regulatory approaches can enhance the effectiveness of regulatory efforts and promote a collective response to global challenges.

In conclusion, privacy, security, and regulatory considerations are critical aspects of CBDC implementation. Balancing privacy and financial transparency, ensuring robust security measures, establishing regulatory frameworks to combat illicit activities, and fostering international cooperation are essential for the successful deployment of CBDCs. By addressing these considerations, central banks can build trust, enhance financial stability, and promote the responsible use of CBDCs in the digital economy.

Chapter 9:

Future Directions and Challenges

Section 1: Exploring the Long-term Implications of CBDCs

Central Bank Digital Currencies (CBDCs) have the potential to shape the future of finance and economies. Understanding the long-term implications of CBDCs is crucial for policymakers, central banks, and stakeholders involved in the financial ecosystem.

1.1 Transforming Financial Systems

CBDCs can transform the way financial systems operate by providing a digital alternative to traditional forms of money. This transformation can lead to increased efficiency, financial inclusion, and new economic opportunities. Exploring the potential impacts on monetary policy, payment systems, and the overall financial infrastructure is vital.

1.2 Reshaping Economic Structures

CBDCs can reshape economic structures by influencing consumption patterns, investment decisions, and the nature of economic transactions. The ability to programmatically embed conditions, such as expiration dates or targeted incentives, in CBDC transactions can have profound effects on economic behavior and policy implementation.

Section 2: The Role of CBDCs in a Digital Economy and the Fourth Industrial Revolution

2.1 Enabling Digital Transformation

CBDCs play a crucial role in a digital economy by providing a secure and efficient means of conducting digital transactions. As the Fourth Industrial Revolution advances, CBDCs can facilitate the integration of emerging technologies such as artificial intelligence, Internet of Things, and decentralized finance, enabling innovative business models and economic growth.

2.2 Promoting Innovation and Financial Services

CBDCs can serve as a platform for innovation, allowing developers and entrepreneurs to build decentralized applications and financial services on top of the CBDC infrastructure. This can foster competition, encourage the development of new financial products and services, and drive economic progress.

Section 3: Addressing Potential Challenges and Risks

3.1 Technological Complexity

The implementation of CBDCs involves navigating complex technological challenges, such as scalability, interoperability, and system resilience. Finding optimal technical solutions, addressing potential bottlenecks, and ensuring the scalability and security of CBDC systems are critical to their successful adoption.

3.2 User Adoption and Acceptance

The widespread adoption of CBDCs relies on user acceptance and trust. Educating the public about the benefits, security measures, and functionality of CBDCs is crucial to foster user confidence. Furthermore, addressing concerns related to privacy, data protection, and usability is essential to encourage the adoption of CBDCs.

Section 4: Evolving Regulatory Frameworks and International Cooperation

4.1 Dynamic Regulatory Frameworks

Regulatory frameworks need to evolve to keep pace with the changing landscape of CBDCs. As CBDCs gain prominence, regulatory authorities must adapt and develop frameworks that address issues such as consumer protection, cybersecurity, cross-border transactions, and market stability. Flexibility, collaboration, and ongoing dialogue between regulators, central banks, and other stakeholders are necessary for effective regulation.

4.2 International Cooperation and Standardization

Given the global nature of CBDCs, international cooperation and standardization efforts are crucial. Establishing common standards, interoperability protocols, and regulatory cooperation frameworks can facilitate cross-border transactions, enhance regulatory compliance, and promote a level playing field.

In conclusion, exploring the long-term implications of CBDCs, understanding their role in a digital economy, addressing potential challenges and risks, and evolving regulatory frameworks are essential for the successful integration of CBDCs into the financial ecosystem. By anticipating future trends, proactively managing risks, and fostering international cooperation, stakeholders can unlock the full potential of CBDCs and navigate the complex landscape of the digital economy.

Chapter 10:
Conclusion

Section 1: Summary of Key Insights and Findings

Throughout this book, we have explored the world of Central Bank Digital Currencies (CBDCs) and delved into various aspects surrounding their introduction, implementation, and implications. Let us summarize the key insights and findings we have uncovered.

1.1 Understanding the Need for Digital Currencies

We examined the need for digital currencies, considering factors such as the changing landscape of financial transactions, financial inclusion, and the potential benefits they offer in terms of efficiency, transparency, and security.

1.2 Evolution of Money and CBDCs

We traced the evolution of money from its early forms to the digital age, recognizing the role of CBDCs in shaping the future of finance. By understanding the historical context, we gained insights into the transformative potential of digital currencies.

1.3 Designing and Implementing CBDCs

We explored the technological foundations of CBDCs, including blockchain and distributed ledger technology, and discussed the advantages, challenges, and alternative approaches to CBDC implementation. We also recognized the importance of legal and

36

regulatory considerations, privacy and security, user adoption, and interoperability in the design and implementation of CBDCs.

1.4 Implications and Challenges

We analyzed the role of central banks in the digital age, assessed the potential benefits and risks of CBDCs, and examined their impact on monetary policy, financial stability, and economic development. We also explored the implications for financial institutions and payment systems, as well as the potential for CBDCs to promote financial inclusion.

1.5 Looking Ahead to the Future

We discussed the future directions and challenges of CBDCs, including their long-term implications, role in a digital economy, addressing potential risks, and evolving regulatory frameworks. By examining these aspects, we gained a deeper understanding of the transformative potential of CBDCs.

Section 2: Looking Ahead to the Future of CBDCs

Looking ahead, the future of CBDCs holds immense possibilities. As technology continues to advance and economies become increasingly digital, CBDCs have the potential to reshape financial systems, promote financial inclusion, and drive economic growth. However, realizing this potential requires careful consideration of various factors, including technological complexities, user adoption, regulatory frameworks, and international cooperation.

Section 3: Final Thoughts on the Transformative Potential of Digital Currencies

In conclusion, digital currencies, particularly CBDCs, have the potential to revolutionize the way we transact, store value, and access financial services. The journey towards widespread CBDC adoption requires collaboration and innovation from central banks, policymakers, financial institutions, technology providers, and society as a whole. By leveraging the transformative potential of CBDCs, we can create more inclusive, efficient, and secure financial systems that benefit individuals, businesses, and economies at large.

As we embark on this digital currency revolution, it is crucial to strike a balance between innovation, security, privacy, and regulatory compliance. By continuously evaluating and adapting to the evolving landscape, we can maximize the benefits and mitigate potential risks associated with CBDCs. The future of finance is digital, and CBDCs are poised to play a significant role in shaping this future.

Let us embrace this transformative potential, working together to build a digital economy that fosters financial inclusion, enhances economic growth, and empowers individuals and communities around the world.

Thank you for purchasing this book!

For additional reading on Blockchain Technology and Cryptocurrency, please check-out my other book:
1. Cryptocurrency Chronicles
   Unlocking The Secrets Of Blockchain Technology

2. A Deep Dive Into The Top 50 Cryptocurrencies
   A DYOR (Do Your Own Research) Guide

3. Common Crypto Investment Pitfalls and How To Avoid
   A DYOR (Do Your Own Research) Guide